Historic England

The Lake District

Billy F. K. Howorth

AMBERLEY

I would like to dedicate Historic England: The Lake District *to my Aunty Sue and Uncle Graham, who have supported and encouraged me to follow my dreams throughout my life.*

First published 2017

Amberley Publishing
The Hill, Stroud, Gloucestershire, GL5 4EP
www.amberley-books.com

Copyright © Billy F. K. Howorth, 2017

The images on the following pages are ©Historic England Archive (Aerofilms Collection): 6, 7 (upper), 8 (lower), 10 (upper), 12, 13 (upper), 14 (upper), 15, 18 (upper), 19, 20, 22–26, 28, 29, 30 (upper), 31, 37, 54, 57, 69 (upper).

The images on the following pages have been reproduced by permission of Historic England Archive: 7 (lower), 10 (lower), 11 (lower), 40, 42, 43, 44 (upper), 45, 47, 48,52, 58, 59, 64, 65, 88 (upper).

The images on the following pages are ©Historic Enlgand Archive: 11 (upper), 14 (lower), 17, 18 (lower), 46, 66, 67, 71, 72, 77–87, 88 (lower), 89–95.

The image on page 27 is ©Historic England Archive. John Laing Collection.

The images on the following pages are © Crown Copyright. Historic England Archive: 70, 73–76.

All other images, unless otherwise stated, are from the author's own collection.

The right of Billy F. K. Howorth to be identified as the Author of this work has been asserted in accordance with the Copyrights, Designs and Patents Act 1988.

ISBN 978 1 4456 7612 8 (print)
ISBN 978 1 4456 7613 5 (ebook)

British Library Cataloguing in Publication Data.
A catalogue record for this book is available from the British Library.

Origination by Amberley Publishing.
Printed in Great Britain.

Contents

Introduction

The Lake District is famed for its high mountain peaks, lush green valleys, and lakes, and is a jewel at the heart of the north-west of England. The history of the Lakes dates to the time of the dinosaurs, when the landscape was dominated by volcanoes, swamps and lagoons. Millions of years later with the arrival of the first humans in the area, we find the first evidence of the landscape being utilised to make various tools and weapons as well as being used for habitation. Later, the northern extent of the Lake District was close to the Roman frontier and Hadrian's Wall. Various forts were constructed around the Lakes, including the important fort Galava in Ambleside, on the banks of Windermere. There were also forts on mountain passes, and the Romans marched down High Street fell.

Throughout the Middle Ages the area still retained it remoteness. Castles and abbeys were constructed across Cumbria and people began to settle around the various lakes. These included the Vikings, who established Above Stock in Ambleside and influenced many place names, and Saxon settlements were established near Askam as well. The settlers came here to farm, which has influenced the landscape we see today.

It was because of the great artists and writers of the eighteenth and nineteenth centuries that the Lake District became better known, with their inspiring paintings and emotive writing revealing the natural beauty of the area to a wider audience. With the advent of rail transportation, people on a mass scale were finally able to explore the area, with the towns of Bowness-on-Windermere, Ambleside, Coniston and Keswick (a train went straight to the town but allowed direct access to the Lakeland experience with the iconic views across Derwentwater) expanding to cater for the new market in tourism.

Today the Lake District retains its wonder, with its stunning panoramas and timeless scenery still drawing tourists from around the world, and more recently in July 2017, the national park was awarded UNESCO World Heritage status. In this book, I have tried to bring together a collection of the most impressive mountains, towns and buildings – both well known and forgotten – that show what the Lake District has to offer, using the archive of Historic England and my own images.

The Lakes

Bassenthwaite Lake

Bassenthwaite Lake located in the north-western part of the Lakes is one of the largest in the Lake District. It is around 4 miles long and ¾ mile wide. Surprisingly the lake is also relatively shallow, dropping to around 70 feet at its deepest point. It is located at the foot of Skiddaw and close to the town of Keswick, and the lake is fed by the River Derwent.

It is also the only lake in the whole of the Lake District to use the word 'Lake' in its title; it has also been known as Bassenwater and Broadwater through history. Today the lake is home to an abundance of wildlife including trout, pike and salmon, as well as cormorants and ospreys, which have been seen fishing in the lake.

Buttermere

Buttermere is located in the west of the Lakes and is 1 ¼ miles long by ¼ mile wide, with a depth of around 75 feet. The nearby village of Buttermere is located on the banks of the lake's north-western shore, with Crummock Water nearby.

It is fed by the River Cocker, which flows through the lake and the nearby Crummock Water to the town of Cockermouth, where it meets the River Derwent. The area surrounding the lake is home to several fells including Fleetwith Pike, Grasmoor, Haystacks and the High Stile. The highlight of Buttermere (and other lakes too) is the gorgeous reflections of the mountains and pines that fringe the lake.

Above and opposite: Coniston Water

Coniston Water is located in the central Lakes, around 6 miles west of Windermere. The lake is the third largest in the Lake District with a length of 5 miles and width of half a mile, with a depth of around 184 feet. It drains into the nearby River Crake and eventually meets the River Leven near the town of Greenodd. It was also known as Thurston Water until the eighteenth century.

The area has been occupied since at least the Bronze Age, with the archaeological remains of farming settlements being uncovered in the area. During the Roman occupation, the fells surrounding the lake were mined for copper and in the later medieval period the area had working iron bloomeries and a potash kiln. The area is often associated with the well-known Brantwood house, the home of John Ruskin from 1872–1900, which is located on the eastern shore of the lake.

The lake is probably most famous for the world water speed records that were set on the lake. In August 1939, Sir Malcolm Campbell travelled at 141.74 mph in his Bluebird K4, setting a world record. Later, his son Donald set four more records between 1956 and 1959 in a Bluebird K7. Sadly, on 4 January 1967, he achieved a top speed of over 320 mph in the Bluebird K7, but on his return leg he lost control. The vehicle crashed and sunk and Donald was killed instantly on impact. The remains of the Bluebird and Campbell were finally recovered in 2001.

Crummock Water

Crummock Water is located in the west between Loweswater and Buttermere. The lake is 2½ miles long and ¾ mile wide, with its deepest point around 140 feet. The northern end of lake is the starting point of the River Cocker and the lake is fed by Scale Force, the tallest waterfall in the Lakes, with a height of around 52 metres.

The lake is also used as a source of water for the nearby towns of Whitehaven, Workington and Maryport. Water is pumped out at the Cornhow treatments works and supplied to the surrounding villages and towns.

Derwentwater

Derwentwater is located in the north-western Lakes and is close to the town of Keswick. The lake is around 3 miles long and 1 mile wide, with a depth of 72 feet. Unusually the lake is both fed and drained by the River Derwent. During the eighteenth and nineteenth centuries, the lake was also known by various other names including the Lake of Derwent, Keswick Water and Keswick Lake. The lake is home to several islands of which only one, Derwent Island, is occupied.

The lake is also a popular destination for tourists and there are boat docks around the island where tourists can hire boats to travel to the surrounding villages including Keswick and Portinscale – known for the iconic views to Catbells and Skiddaw.

Ennerdale Water
Ennerdale Water is the most westerly
lake close to the port of Whitehaven.
It is around 2½ miles long and 1 mile
wide, and is relatively deep with a
depth of 150 feet. The lake is fed by
the River Liza and drains into the
River Ehen.

Through the centuries it has also
been referred to as Brodewater,
Brodwater, Broad Water, and
Ennerdale Lake. Importantly the lake
is in the Ennerdale Valley, which has
some of the Lake District's best-known
mountains including High Crag,
Green Cable, Great Gable and Pilllar.
Pillar's slopes fall directly down to
the lake and the view across the lake
with Pillar behind is one of the little-
known stunning views in the whole
Lake District.

Esthwaite Water

Esthwaite Water is one of the smallest lakes and is located in the south Lakeland, between Coniston Water and Windermere, with the village of Hawkshead located to the north of the lake.

The lake is one of the least known in the Lakes and covers a small area of around 280 acres. It is notable because it is home to many species of fish including pike and trout, and it has gained a reputation as a fishing hotspot. Due its nutrient-rich waters that support a huge variety of water-dwelling plants, the lake has been designated as a Site of Special Scientific Interest.

Grasmere

Grasmere is located in the central Lakes and is one of the smallest lakes. It is located between the village of Grasmere and Rydal Water. The lake is around 1 mile long and almost half a mile wide with its deepest point at 70 feet. Like the nearby Rydal Water, the lake is both fed and drained by the River Rothay, which flows through Grasmere into Rydal Water and on to Windermere.

The lake is also home to a singular island, known simply as The Island. In a usual quirk of history, this island was originally sold in 1893 to a private bidder. It was local Canon Hardwicke Drummond Rawnsley who believed that the island should have instead been retained for use by the public and was so incensed by the decision that he went on to become a founding member of the National Trust. In 2017 the island was gifted back to the National Trust. The famous local poet William Wordsworth moved to Grasmere in 1799 and his work – and other Romantic poets – helped immortalise the Lake District.

Haweswater

Haweswater is one of only a handful of man-made reservoir lakes. It is around 4 miles long and half a mile wide, and is located on the site of an earlier natural lake that was around 2½ miles long. The current lake was expanded further in 1929 when the Haweswater dam was constructed by the Manchester Corporation.

The dam was built in the Mardale Valley and caused an outcry from the residents and farmers, whose land and villages would be flooded. In 1935, just before the valley was flooded, all the houses and farms in the villages of Mardale Green and Measand were demolished. The local village church was dismantled and reused in the construction. In addition to this all the bodies in the graveyard were excavated and reinterred in the village of Shap.

Upon completion, the dam measured 470 metres long and around 27 metres high; it also increased the water level by 29 metres once the reservoir filled with water. At full capacity it can hold around 84 billion litres of water and supplies around 25 per cent of the water used in the north-west.

Above and opposite: Rydal Water

Rydal Water is located in the central Lakes and is one of the smallest lakes. It is located between Grasmere lake and Windermere, close to the hamlet of Rydal. The lake is ¾ mile long and around ¼ mile wide, with a depth of 65 feet. The lake is fed by the River Rothay, which flows from Grasmere through Rydal Water and downstream to Windermere. It was previously known as Routhmere.

Unusually the lake is owned by two different groups. The northern extent is part of the Rydal Hall estate and is reserved for the residents of the hall, whereas the southern extent is leased by the Lowther estate to the National Trust. The western edge of the lake is home to the feature known as Wordworth's Seat, considered to be the favourite vantage point of the poet.

Thirlmere

Thirlmere is a reservoir located between Keswick and Grasmere. It is 3 ¾ miles long and 0.1 mile wide with a depth of around 131 feet. It is located on the site of an earlier lake known by other names including Leathes Water, Wythburn Water and Thirle Water.

In 1863 a pamphlet urged that Thirlmere and Haweswater should be made into reservoirs, and their water transported to provide London with a source of clean water. Later, in 1875, John Frederick Bateman suggested that Manchester and Liverpool could jointly use water from Haweswater and Ullswater for their supplies, but due to disagreements this did not happen.

It was the Manchester Corporation who decided to construct a dam at the northern end, creating a reservoir that provided Manchester with a supply of water via the Thirlmere Aqueduct. After a series of delays the dam was officially opened in 1894 and the reservoir and the aqueduct are still used to provide water to the Manchester area to this day. The historic view of the former lakes, Wythburn Water and Leathes Water, looking north before the dam is a magical image and makes you appreciate the damage that the reservoir caused.

Ullswater

Ullswater is located in the north-eastern Lakes and is the second largest in the Lake District, with a length of around 9 miles and width of ¾ mile, and a depth of around 197 feet. The river drains into the River Eamont to the north.

The lake is one of the most popular and least populated of the lakes, linked to the central Lakes by the Kirkstone Pass. The area is cut off by the continuous high range of mountains to both the east and west. On the edge of the lake is the village of Glenridding to the south and Pooley Bridge to the north. Helvellyn is located close by and on the eastern side of the lake is the impressive waterfall known as Aira Force.

Ullswater is a lake of astonishing elemental beauty, and the most like a Scottish loch. At the head of the valley the mountains form an arresting backdrop and fall steeply into the lake.

Above and opposite: Windermere

Windermere is the largest natural lake in England and has been one of the most popular tourist destinations for almost 150 years. The lake is the longest in the Lake District; however, there is a debate as to whether the stretch of water between Newby Bridge and Lakeside should be considered as part of Windermere, or part of the River Leven.

The lake is 11 ¼ miles long if measured from the bridge at Newby Bridge and is almost 1 mile wide, with a maximum depth of 219 feet. It is fed by the rivers Brathay, Rothay, Trout Beck and Cunsey Beck and is drained by the River Leven to the south. The lake encompasses eighteen islands, the largest of which is Belle Isle, close to Bowness-on-Windermere. The lake was also known as Winander Mere and Winandermere until the nineteenth century.

Around Windermere

Above and opposite: The Lakeside, Bowness-on-Windermere

The area beside the lake is one of the most well-known parts of Bowness-on-Windermere. Here you find the docks for the steamers and the quintessential buildings of the Victorian waterside. This part of the town and lakeside is dominated by the imposing Belsfield Hotel, which was originally a house designed by George Webster and later became a hotel in 1890.

This part of the lakeside is also home to the Windermere Ferry, which has been connecting Ferry Nab to Far Sawrey on the western side of the lake for hundreds of years, a journey which takes around ten minutes.

Above, right and opposite: Town Centre, Bowness-on-Windermere The centre of the town, a short distance from the lakeside, is a maze of small streets with a main route that travels uphill to the nearby town of Windermere. One of the oldest buildings in the town is St Martin's Church, which was built in 1483 on the foundations of an earlier church.

Originally, the town was a small fishing village, but since the Victorian period it has become a tourist hotspot, helped by its location on the lake and the nearby railway in Windermere. Many hotels and business have grown and expanded in the town due to its popularity.

Above and opposite: Sailing on Windermere

For centuries the lake has been home to boats. The famous Windermere Ferry has been operating for at least 500 years, transporting people from one side to the other. Later, pleasure steamers became a popular attraction, partly due to the new railways that were serving the area, and a few of these can still be seen today including the *Tern*, *Teal* and *Swan*. Nowadays there is also a water bus service that operates on the lake.

Sailing for pleasure is also a popular pastime and there are several boat clubs around Windermere. The lake also served as the location for a world water speed record when, in June 1930, Sir Henry Segrave broke the world water speed record in his boat *Miss England II*, which travelled at speed of 98.76 mph. Unfortunately, on his third run the boat capsized. His mechanic, Victor Helliwell, drowned but Segrave was rescued. Due to his injuries, he passed away shortly afterwards, but he is remembered as one of the few people to have held both the world land speed and water speed records simultaneously. Later during the 1950s, Norman Buckley also set several world water speed records on the lake.

Above and opposite: Belle Isle, Bowness-on-Windermere

The island is the largest on Windermere and has been occupied since Roman times. During the Roman occupation, the island was home to a villa constructed for the Roman governor in nearby Ambleside and was later a Royalist stronghold during the Civil War. It was originally known by several names including Great Island, Long Holme and Longholm.

The most important development of the island was in 1774 when the impressive Belle Isle House (noted as the first house built purely for the picturesque quality of its surroundings, according to Wordsworth) was constructed by the Curwen family and the island was named after their daughter Isabella. Unusually, the house is a circular building, three storeys tall and has an elaborate portico, reminiscent of the Pantheon in Rome. Later, in 1781 the house was sold to Isabella and the house and island were permanently renamed after her. Subsequent generations of the Curwen family lived on the island until 1993, when the house was sold.

Town Centre, Windermere

Windermere is located around half a mile from the town of Bowness-on-Windermere at the top of a hill. The town is a very popular destination for visitors who enjoy exploring the town and its unique centre. The town was originally known as Birthwaite before the arrival of the Kendal & Windermere Railway, which opened in 1847 and is still in service, connecting Windermere with Kendal and Oxenholme, and then connecting on to the West Coast mainland.

One of the town's most imposing buildings is the Windermere Hotel, originally known as the Riggs Windermere Hotel. The hotel opened at the same time as the railways and still serves as a hotel today.

Ambleside

Ambleside is the most northerly town on the edge of Windermere, and has retained its traditional Lakeland character, becoming a popular tourist destination with a wide range of shops, pubs, restaurants and hotels.

It is also a common base for mountaineers, hikers and bikers wishing to explore the central Lakes. The town is served by the nearby steamers, which moor at Waterhead, around 1 mile from the town centre.

Waterhead, Ambleside

To the northern end of Windermere lies Waterhead, a small cluster of hotels, houses and a boat dock that serve as Ambleside's connection to the rest of Windermere. Waterhead is home to a stopping point for the Windermere steamers, which connect Ambleside to Bowness-on-Windermere and Lakeside.

The area's most important archaeological site is the Roman fort of Galava, the remains of which can still be seen today in a nearby field. The fort was originally constructed during the Roman occupation around AD 79 and was used to protect the trade routes that ran through the Lake District from the northern frontier. The site was excavated between 1914 and 1920 by R. G. Collingwood, who unearthed the remains of the main gate, granaries and various other buildings with the artefacts discovered during the excavation still on display at Kendal Museum.

Above, right and overleaf: Town Centre, Ambleside

The Ambleside town centre with its twisting maze of streets and alleys makes it a quintessential Lakeland town, with the buildings constructed using local materials including slate. One of the well-known buildings in the town is the Bridge House, a seventeenth-century structure originally built by the Braithwaite family so that they could access their land on the other side of Stock Beck as well as provide a place to store apples from their orchards.

Over the centuries it has been used as a weaving shop, a tearoom, a cobblers shop and also as a home for a family of eight people. It was restored after fundraising efforts by the locals during the 1920s and ensured the survival of this unique building (National Trust have also played a part and now own it). Not far from the Bridge House you can also find a replica waterwheel, located at the former Bark Mill, which manufactured wooden bobbins for the textile industry.

Above and opposite: Newby Bridge

Newby Bridge is a small farming hamlet located at the southernmost reach of Windermere on the River Leven. It is best known for its stone bridge, which crosses the river and the adjoining Swan Hotel.

   Close by is Lakeside, the final stopping point for the Lakeside & Haverthwaite Railway, which was originally a branch line for the Furness Railway. It closed in 1965 and reopened in 1973. Lakeside is also a stopping point for the popular Windermere steamers, which provide a service across the lake to Bowness-on-Windermere and other locations around the lake.

Above and opposite: Swan Hotel, Newby Bridge

The imposing and famous hotel known as the Swan Hotel stands on the site of an original dwelling dating to around 1623. In the later eighteenth century, the building underwent alterations and was extended.

The building sits on the picturesque banks of the River Leven close to the southernmost extent of Windermere and on the main transport route between Barrow, Ulverston and Kendal. The hotel is accessible by the stone bridge, which allows access to the northern side of the river, the nearby Lakeside, and the western side of the lake.

Lakeland Towns and Villages

Above and opposite: Coniston

Coniston is a small village located between Coniston Water and the peak known as Coniston Old Man. The village was originally founded due to farming in the area and also served as a hub for the local slate and copper mines that were in operation. During the Victorian period, the town rapidly developed a reputation as a tourist destination and was serviced by the Coniston brand of the Furness Railway, which opened in 1859. The town has also become well known for its local resident John Ruskin, who bought the nearby Brantwood house. During the 1920s the village was powered by pioneering hydroelectric power; however, the residents were asked to pay so heavily through taxes that they were forced to return to the national grid. In more recent times the town and nearby lake were known for the water speed records that were set during the twentieth century.

Above and opposite: Hawkshead

Hawkshead is a small village located to the north of Esthwaite Water. The town has a strong tradition of farming and was originally part of the lands owned by Furness Abbey. During the medieval period the town developed and hosted a wool market, later developing into an important market town in 1608.

One of the oldest surviving buildings is the Hawkshead Grammar School, which was founded in 1585 and eventually closed in 1909. During the eighteenth and nineteenth centuries, the town grew in importance. Poet William Wordsworth went to the grammar school and writer Beatrix Potter lived near the village with her husband during the early twentieth century.

Glenridding

Glenridding is a popular destination for walkers and climbers wanting to tackle Helvellyn and is located at the southern end of Ullswater. The town is quite small with a few hotels and hostels and is well known for being home to the Ullswater steamers, which operate on the lake between Glenridding and Pooley Bridge.

The area was once home to Greenside Mine, one of the largest lead mines in the Lake District. Ore was first discovered in the eighteenth century and the site was in use until its closure in 1962 – it was due to the mine that the town developed around the site. More recently the town was devastated by severe flooding during Storm Desmond in December 2015, with many businesses and homes being badly damaged.

Above and overleaf: Keswick

The town of Keswick, located to the north of Derwentwater, has been an important market town since the Middle Ages, when it was granted a market charter by Edward I in 1276. The town was first recorded during the thirteenth century; however, evidence points to much earlier occupation of the area in prehistoric times and the Roman occupation, as well as during the time of the Tudors, when the town became an important hub for mining in the area.

The town was opened up to tourism for the first time during the eighteenth century with the creation of turnpikes that ran throughout the Lakes. These allowed for the routes to be improved and more tourists to visit the area. Later, in the nineteenth century the town was serviced by the Cockermouth, Keswick & Penrith Railway, which began its service in 1865, with the route finally closing in 1972.

The town's best-known building is the Moot Hall, which was rebuilt in 1813 and stands in the middle of the main street. The town is also famous for its pencil manufacturing, which originally started as a small-scale industry and later grew into a major industry in the area.

The Mountains

Above: Cat Bells

Cat Bells is one of the smallest fells in the Lakes with a height of 451 metres and is located around 3 miles from Keswick. Due to its modest height, it is one of the most popular climbs in the Lakes, as it is easily accessible to most people, including families. It is also popular because it is the highlight of the iconic westerly view across the lake and because it is easily reached by steamers across the lake from Keswick.

It is also home to the Yewthwaite mine, which is located on the western side, but the large spoil heaps and shafts make this part of the fell dangerous to visitors. On the eastern side you can also find the Brandlehow and Old Brandley mine. All of the mines around Cat Bells closed during the 1890s.

Opposite: Blencathra

Blencathra is one of the most northern mountains in the Lakes, and has six separate fell tops, the highest of which is the Hallsfell Top, which has a height of 868 metres.

It is possible to view many of the peaks in the Lakes from the summit including Helvellyn, Scafell Pike, Great Gable and Coniston Old Man, as well as the distant Cheviot Hills, Forest of Bowland and, on a clear day, the Isle of Man and North Wales. The lakes of Derwent Water and Thirlmere can also be seen from the summit.

Above, below and opposite: Helvellyn

Helvellyn is the third tallest mountain in the Lake District and England with its peak reaching 950 metres, and forms part of the Helvellyn range. The mountain is a favourite with climbers and is famous for its route across Striding Edge, which involves some scrambling. Due to the nature of this feature it has become a well-known accident hotspot.

Strangely, the former county boundary between Cumberland and Westmorland lay along the length of the Helvellyn Ridge, meaning that the summit of Helvellyn was the highest point in Westmorland. The mountain is also famous for an unusual flying feat, when in 1926 a small aircraft landed and then took off from the summit.

Above and opposite: The Kirkstone Pass

One of the most impressive routes through the Lakes is the Kirkstone Pass, which takes visitors from the banks of Windermere across the high fells to Ullswater. The mountain pass rises to a height of 454 metres and is notable for its old coaching inn. The pass is named after the boulder located close to the inn, which is said to resemble the steeple of a church, with the word 'kirk' meaning 'church' in the Old Norse language.

The route from Ambleside to the Kirkstone Pass is known as 'The Struggle' due to its series of tight bends and narrowing route, as well as the difficulty it poses during the winter when it is often inaccessible.

Above and opposite: Scafell Pike

Scafell Pike is the tallest mountain in the Lake District and England, with its peak reaching 978 metres. It forms part of the south fells according to Wainwright, although some would argue Scafell Pike is in the west. Usually, the mountain is also home to the highest standing body of water in England and is known as Broad Crag Tarn, located at a height of around 820 metres.

In 1919 the summit of Scafell Pike was donated to the National Trust by Lord Leconfield in memory of the men of the Lakes who died fighting during the First World War. Today the mountain is one of the peaks that forms part of the National Three Peaks Challenge, the other being Ben Nevis and Snowdon.

Great Gable

Great Gable is one of the most popular mountains in the Lake District, and its peak reaches 899 metres. Located in the western fells, the range occupies a triangular section of the Lakes and is bordered by the River Cocker and Wasdale. The summit of the mountain is covered with boulders and the highest point is marked by a rock outcrop set with a cairn.

In 1924 members of the Fell and Rock Climbing Club bought 3,000 acres of land including the mountain and donated it to the National Trust. The club installed a memorial plaque on the summit that is dedicated to the members of the club who died fighting in the First World War.

Skiddaw

Skiddaw, located just to the north of Keswick, is one of the tallest mountains in the Lake District, with its peak reaching 931 metres. It is also the sixth highest mountain in England. It lends its name to the nearby Skiddaw Forest as well as the Skiddaw slate that is mined in the area.

The summit has several tops, which are known as North Top, Middle Top, South Top and High Man, which is considered the actual summit. From the summit it is possible on a clear day to see the Cheviots Hills and the North Pennines, the Helvellyn range and Coniston Fells as well as the Isle of Man and Solway Firth.

Wansfell

Wansfell is situated close to the town of Ambleside at the northern end of Windermere.

It is notable for its summit ridge, which has two peaks; the higher of the two is Baystones, standing at 488 metres, although the nearby Wansfell Pike is 482 metres and is considered by most walkers to be the true summit due to its greater vantage point.

The fell forms part of the southern ridge of Caudale Moor and covers the area between Ambleside and the Troutbeck valley. Wansfell is very popular with walkers in Ambleside and is closely linked to the town.

Houses and Monuments

Above and overleaf: Brantwood

The house is famous for being the home of John Ruskin, the Victorian art critic and artist. At the end of the eighteenth century, Thomas Woodville constructed a small house on the site and the house and its estate underwent expansion around 1833.

The house was home to many interesting characters over the years including William James Linton, artist and social reformer, and Gerald Massey, poet and Egyptologist. In 1871 the house was bought by Ruskin. Upon his purchase of the house, he arranged for the house to be repaired and altered. He decorated his house with art, including paintings by Turner and Gainsborough, as well as a large collection of minerals and sea shells.

In 1878 a new dining room was built at the south end of the house, and a second storey was constructed around 1890. Upon his death in 1900, the house and estate were inherited by the Severn family and he expressed in his will that the house should be open for thirty days a year for visitors to see his house and collection. Unfortunately, his wishes were not granted and the family sold off many of the pictures.

After the death of Arthur Severn in 1931, all the remaining contents were auctioned. Ruskin's last pupil, Emily Warren, prompted a successful drive to have the house made into a museum. The house was bought by John Howard Whitehouse, founder of Bembridge School and of the Birmingham Ruskin Society. He also established the Brantwood Trust in 1951.

Dove Cottage

Close to the village of Grasmere you find Dove Cottage, the former home of William Wordsworth. It was built during the seventeenth century on the main route between Ambleside and Keswick and originally housed an inn named the Dove & Olive, which eventually closed in 1793. The building was constructed using local stone and slate and houses four rooms on each floor.

Wordsworth first came across the building in 1799 while walking in the Lakes with his close friend Samuel Taylor Coleridge. He wanted to find a place where he could reconnect with his sister Dorothy, whom he had grown distant from. The house was vacant and he decided to rent it for the sum of £5 per year.

When he married his wife Mary in 1802, she and her sister Sara joined William and Dorothy at the cottage. Afterwards, Mary gave birth to three children – John, Dora and Thomas. Eventually the family outgrew the cottage and moved in 1808, making way for new resident Thomas de Quincey, the famous writer. The cottage was purchased in 1890 by the Wordsworth Trust, who opened it to visitors a year later.

Above and opposite: Grizedale Hall

One of the most notable houses that has now been lost was Grizedale Hall, located in Grizedale Forest. There had been a hall on the site since the seventeenth century, when the Rawlinson family acquired the estate in 1614.

In 1745 Richard Ford built a new home, known as Ford Lodge, on part of the estate. His great-grandson Montague Ainslie, who inherited the estate in the nineteenth century, turned the lodge into a larger residence in 1841, which became known as Grizedale New Hall. In 1903, Harold Brocklebank, a merchant from Liverpool, purchased the estate. He demolished the old hall and completely rebuilt it in the neo-Gothic style in 1905, naming it Grizedale Hall. The family lived at the hall until his death in 1936, when the hall and estate fell under the control of the Forestry Commission.

Unusually, during the Second World War the hall was commandeered by the War Office and used as a prisoner of war camp. The site was known as No.1 POW Camp (Officers) Grizedale Hall, and was used to house the most senior German officers. The camp closed in 1946. Sadly, after this period the house stood empty and due to the high upkeep costs, all the internal fittings were auctioned off. The house was eventually demolished in 1957. Today some of the remains of the hall can still be seen, including the large garden terrace.

Above and opposite: Rayrigg Hall

Rayrigg Hall is one of the little-known houses in the Lake District, with the earliest parts dating back centuries. The house, with its imposing façade, is one of the hidden gems of the Lakes.

The grounds also house an original courtyard, which includes a stable, barns and old coach house. The house is probably most famous for hosting abolitionist William Wilberforce during his summer visits to the Lake District.

Storrs Hall

The hall is one of the most prominent and well known on the banks of Windermere. The house was built in the 1790s by Sir John Legard, a prominent landowner from Yorkshire. He sold the house due to ill health in 1804 to John Bolton, who made his fortune in the Liverpool slave trade. The house was extended and he also created a park in the surrounding land.

The house was used as a place to entertain friends and family, and he became well known for hosting regattas on Windermere, which were attended by prominent people of the time including William Wordsworth and Sir Walter Scott. Upon his death, the house passed to Elizabeth Bolton, who passed it on to Revd Thomas Staniforth, her nephew, who resided at the house until 1887.

After his death, and with no heirs, the house was sold off. From 1940 to 1944 it hosted the staff and boys of St Hugh's School, Woodhall Spa, who had been evacuated from Lincolnshire during the Second World War. In the present day the hall has been preserved and is now a hotel.

Wray Castle

Wray Castle is one of the most impressive structures in the Lake District, located close to the western edge of Windermere. It was constructed in 1840 by James Dawson, a surgeon from Liverpool. The structure is built in a neo-Gothic style, and at the same time he also built the nearby Wray Church.

Upon his death in 1875, the house passed on to his nephew Edward Preston, and only two years later passed to Edward's cousin, Hardwicke Rawnsley, who was also the vicar at the adjoining Wray Church. In 1929 the castle was given to the National Trust by Sir Robert Noton Barclay and has been used for various purposes including a youth hostel, offices for the Freshwater Biological Association and as a Merchant Navy training college from 1958–98. Since 2011 it has been once again opened to visitors.

Above, opposite and overleaf: Castlerigg Stone Circle

One of the most impressive prehistoric sites in the Lakes is the inspiring stone circle at Castlerigg, near Keswick. The site is believed to date to around 3200 BC and may be one of the earliest constructed in Britain. It is sometimes referred to as Druids' Circle.

There are thirty-eight stones made of slate, set in a circular pattern around 32 metres at the widest point and 30 metres at the narrowest. Some estimates suggest that the heaviest stone weighs an impressive 16 tons, with the tallest stone measuring just over 2 metres in height.

On the northern side there is a gap in the stones, which is suggested to be a possible entrance. One of the most unusual differences is that this circle has a rectangle of standing stones within it. The only known excavation at the site was undertaken by W. K. Dover in 1882, and the site was among sixty-eight sites listed for protection in the Ancient Monuments Protection Act 1882.

Industry in the Lakes

Above and overleaf: Honister Slate Mine

The slate mine is one of the best-preserved examples of a slate mine the in Lakes and is famous for the mining of Westmorland green slate. The area has been quarried for its slate since 1728, with opencast quarrying occurring at the site since the seventeenth century. But as demand grew, mining was increasingly done underground.

By the mid-nineteenth century the mine had stretched underneath Honister Crag, with a smaller mine operating on the other side of the valley at Yew Crags. In 1879 the mine owners also leased several additional quarries and at the same time installed a self-acting incline at the Honister and Yew Crags mines, which allowed slate to be moved easier and quicker.

In 1891, production at the mine had reached 3,000 tons a year with more than 100 employees. The mines ceased production during the First World War due to employee shortages, but work quickly resumed shortly afterwards. The mine once again underwent an enforced closure from 1943–45.

By 1981 all the quarries of the Buttermere & Westmorland Green Slate Co. Ltd. were purchased by B. R. Moore, who undertook new investment and regeneration including battery locomotives, new rolling stock and specialist machinery for underground mining. Between 1985 and 1989, it was owned by Alfred McAlpine plc until its closure. The mine was finally reopened in 1997 and produces roofing slate while at the same time becoming a tourist attraction.

Kirkstone Slate Quarry

Slate mining has always been an important industry in the Lake District and mines can be found throughout the area. In the area close to Kirkstone Pass you can find the Kirkstone slate quarry, famed for its Kirkstone green slate. This site has been quarried for over 100 years.

Over the decades the site was owned by various companies and the Kirkstone Quarries business, which was established in 1949. Unfortunately, due to changes in mining and importing goods, the quarry became unprofitable and was closed down in 2012.

Above, opposite and overleaf: Bonsor Copper Mine

The area around Coniston was known for its copper mines, which, owing to the way the copper was deposited, meant that the mines had to be cut very deep, sometimes to around 1,600 feet. It has been suggested that the industry first started around 1563 when experts from Germany arrived in the area.

In 1568 the Company of Mines Royal was founded and in 1590 they discovered copper veins at Coniston. These were mined continuously until the Civil War in 1642, after which the industry seemed to have declined.

It was during the early eighteenth century that the copper mines were once again exploited and in 1758 the Macclesfield Copper Co. was formed and mined the Bonsor Vein at Coniston. By 1795 the mine had reached a depth of around 300 feet. It was abandoned when the owners decided that digging deeper would be unproductive.

In 1824, John Taylor, the famous mining engineer, came to Coniston with the aim of making the mines into the largest and most profitable in the north. The mines were so productive that in 1858 it was decided to construct a branch line on the Furness Railway to allow the ore to be transported more easily. In the later part of the nineteenth century production output began to reduce and upkeep costs were increasing. With the importation of cheaper foreign ore in the 1880s, the fate of the Lakeland mines was sealed. Over the next few years the mines closed and were left to decay, providing us today with a window into the lost industry of the Lakes.

Above and overleaf: The Derwent Cumberland Pencil Co.

The Derwent Cumberland Pencil Co. was founded in 1832 as Banks, Son & Co. and their pencils were manufactured by hand in a small workshop. But with increased mechanisation, the business developed. Over the subsequent decades the business was sold serval times and in 1916 it was renamed the Cumberland Pencil Co.

Their products are known worldwide and are famously sold in tins. Derwent's oldest product line of colour pencils, known as Artist, was expanded from twenty-four to seventy-two colours in 1939 and again from seventy-two to 120 colours in 1996. The company is best known as being the supplier of the pencils that were used in the animated 1982 film *The Snowman*.

Lakeland Life

Above and overleaf: Rural Life

Up until the mid-twentieth century there were still many remote communities and settlements scattered across the Lake District. These settlements had survived over the centuries by relying on the land to provide the inhabitants with everything they needed.

One of the biggest industries of farming, an industry which is still important to Lakeland life in the modern day. The surviving images of these small communities give us useful insight into the past and show us what life was like for the residents of these rural communities throughout the nineteenth and twentieth centuries.

Cattle Farming
Another important industry in the Lake District is cattle farming. These farms provided not only a plentiful supply of meat, but also a source of hides that could be utilised by the tanning and leather manufacturing industries.

Although it is not as common as sheep farming, this industry forms one of the backbones of farming throughout the Lakes.

Above and opposite: Sheep Farming

Sheep farming has always been one of the traditional farming industries in the Lakes. Sheep were bred for their wool, which was then sold at the local charter markets. Their meet was also sold, which provided a much-needed income.

The Lake District is probably most famous for the Herdwick sheep, a native of the Lakes and an animal well adapted to the harsh environment. Their wool is unique due to its durability and thick fibres – perfect for acting as a layer of insulation.

Left and opposite: Hunting One of the most important activities undertaken over hundreds of years in the Lakes is hunting. The landscape allows for an abundance of wildlife to thrive in the environment, from rabbits and foxes to deer. The Lakes also provide a home to birdlife including ducks and geese.

Over the years the methods of hunting have changed, with hounds no longer being used in the same way. Hunting has been an important part of many local villages, with people of all generations getting involved.

Traditional Crafts

The remoteness of many of the
Lakeland villages over the
centuries meant that the local
population had to be
self-sufficient in providing
their own resources. Local
materials were used to build
houses and barns, wood
was used to make baskets,
carts and bobbins, and local
stone and slate were used to
construct buildings, bridges
and walking routes.

This seclusion from the wider
area has allowed the Lakes
to develop its own distinctive
character, much of which
can still be seen today and is
popular with visiting tourists.

Right and overleaf: Walking in the Lakes

For hundreds of years the Lake District has been drawing people from all over Britain and around the world to its craggy peaks and lush valleys. The landscape of the Lakes has been a tourist attraction for people of all ages and abilities who wish to unlock the secrets of the Lakes and experience some of the most impressive views and panoramas imaginable.

The Lake District and its mountains were arguably most popularised by Alfred Wainwright, who undertook the task of recording 214 mountains and fells in his series of pictorial guides to the Lakes. Today the Lake District remains a popular destination for climbers, walkers and mountain bikers wishing to explore the area. The Lake District recently became a World Heritage site, joining iconic locations such as the Taj Mahal, the Great Barrier Reef and Grand Canyon as a place of international acclaim.